Lucid Waking

Insight Cards

First published in Australia in 2025
By Jessica Berry

Text and illustrations copyright 2024
by Jessica Berry
This book is copyright. Apart from any fair dealing for the purposes of private study, research, criticism, or review permitted under the Copyright Act 1968, no part may be reproduced by any process without prior written permission from the author.

National Library of Australia
Cataloguing-in-Publication data:
Berry, Jessica, 2025, author, illustrator
Lucid Waking Insight cards/ Jessica Berry
author and illustrator
ISBN 978-0-646-70955-0

Design by Jessica berry
Printed by Ingram Spark

Contents

Welcome 3
This is not a tarot deck 4
Lucid Waking 5
How to read the cards 7

The Cards

Origin 11
Attention 15
Sovereignty 19
Integrity 23
Surrender 25
Lucid Waking 27
Contrast 31
Wisdom 35
Seeking 37
Suffering 41
Cycles 45
Support 47
Innocence 49
Earth 51
Vibration 53
Resonance 57
Rebirth 61
Gratitude 63
Poems 65

Welcome

Welcome to the Lucid Waking insight card deck! I am thrilled and grateful that you have decided to engage with my creation, it has been created with the sole purpose of bringing benefit to those who encounter it. If you don't resonate with the insight I am sharing then throw it out and move on, this is your journey.

This book and accompanying card deck are the culmination of a life spent deep in what I call 'spiritual nerding'. I have had a life's passion to understand what the hell is going on here on Earth. As a young person I wanted to know 'what is the point of this apparent realm of suffering?' My research has taken many forms, I have read and listened and lived and lost and got into all sorts of scrapes and triumphs. I am eternally grateful to all my teachers; both those who are aware they are teachers and those who were unaware. I have learned a lot from the many challenges I have faced and the experience of rising to these challenges has deepened my capacity to continue my expansion wholeheartedly.

If you are still mad at 'God' you may find this work challenging as my spiritual nerd journey has led me to a deep and abiding knowing of myself as a fractal emanation of the Divine Source. I have fun coming up with all sorts of names for the un-nameable and you will encounter many of them in this work. I don't use the term 'God' personally because of all the baggage tied to that word that doesn't cut it when attempting to give a definition to the Undefinable.

My life's project (obsession) has led me to voyage into a fairly exhaustive myriad of forms of human wisdom and meaning making systems. I'm like the detective in that iconic scene in detective movies with the red thread interlinking all the evidence. I do not subscribe to any one system of human meaning making and never will. I have benefited from all the wisdom I have encountered. This work is my unique response to the masterful pillars of Knowing that have come before me. Once I became consciously intimate with Source I understood it was my own Expanded Self who discerned whether or not what I researched and strove to understand resonated as Truth. I understand this of you too. Some pillars of wisdom I have studied are foundational in the making of this work and they are as follows: The Wisdom of the Buddha, The Vedanta of Advaita ,The Loving Mastery of Jesus, The Way of Tao, The mysticism of the Sufis, The Hermetic Principles and The Law of One. The whisperings of Mother Gaia guide me always.

This is not a Tarot Deck

Some of the universal human soul archetypes I have collated for this deck certainly have counterparts in the tarot, but it is not a tarot deck. Though I do often have the nickname 'The Oracle' I also don't call this an oracle deck. I purposely call it an Insight deck. I want to convey that all wisdom emanates from Within. If you truly resonate with a teaching it is your inner knowing that brings this resonance. In this way we can also use the term 'divination' as it is for the purpose of connecting to the Divine expansion that we use these cards. I offer this book and card deck as a companion to accessing your own expanded insight. Often we call this expanded self the Higher self. I don't mind this as a name but I want to point to the nature of the expanded reality as non hierarchical. The human personality self is just as much an intrinsic part of the greater weaving of the infinite tapestry as any more expanded awareness we 'remember' into. I affectionately call this higher or expanded self 'You with a better view'. We can testify it is certainly not always easy to hear the gps system of the higher self because things can really get complex down here on ground zero. The incessant racket of clamouring bullshit down here serves to drown out the majestic love letters from the Divine that we are eternally being sent. The path to mastery includes learning how to turn one's attention from the clamouring bollocks to the sparkling truth. There are no card reversals. If you feel triggered by a card it is an opportunity to release stored energy that you are ready to expand beyond. Let yourself feel your authentic feelings and responses, you are loved by an Infinity that made you and no one with any real authority will ever judge you. It is a fun game of mine to question the authority of my critical thoughts. I say "mmhmm and who are you?".

Lucid Waking

I see this current epoch on Earth as the mass awakening from what I call 'the game of winners and losers' and the return to Unity consciousness. Lucid waking is to be awake while awake. We wake up from the dream of the game of winners and losers. The new game we are loading is Unity consciousness. Its very exciting! I was born tired of this stinky old ruthless strategy game. I know my Divine Porpoise is to co-create the new world based on the Law of One. I have created this book and card deck as akin to a pocket guide to communicating with the expanded self. Each card will act as a key to bring forth what lays currently in your subconscious, or it will bring an emphasis of what you are very much aware of in this now.

How to read the cards

I believe in the intimacy of this experience of the Divine AS me. Each one of us dances a unique dance with Spirit and all are valid. In this way your own wisdom is the best wisdom for you. Begin your reading by connecting in to your own Higher or Expanded guidance. You can do this simply by asking for it in whatever way feels natural to you. I like to place my hand on my heart centre. There are absolutely no rules as to how to choose and lay out your cards. The experience of surrendering to your intuition on this will benefit you deeply. All cards represent the Now. Even if you are asking for insight into the past or future, your expanded self lives in the timeless Now. All insights are a reflection of your experience in this now moment. Everything is in a dynamic state of flux and flow. Each time you do a reading will be a fresh and living message. As you become familiar with the cards over time I recommend you remain open to new insights you may not have understood before. Although I have provided this book as guidance for the cards, I want to emphasise that the message you receive from the cards is unique to your own wisdom and insight. I absolutely love doing private readings with people because

I benefit from the unique wisdoms of everyone I read for. It is a delight to see my creation serving the people I read for. If the idea of a reading with me interests you do get in touch, my intuition is very honed and helpful and the collaborations between your higher self and mine are always wonderful because I benefit from the unique wisdoms of everyone I read for. It is a delight to see my creation serving the people I read for.

Connect with me: @kundalinguini_

The Cards

Origin

The Origin card signifies The Eye of the I. The Portal of All Creation. Our Infinite Source is a Fullness that can also be understood as Emptiness because any attempt to make a definition of the All will lead to the understanding that an Infinite Consciousness must be indefinable.

The fun irony here is that even this definition you are reading right now will merely point to the Unspeakable Knowing in which we are all Known. I always say 'It's the ineffable innit'. This is because the Source is the Origin of

Ultimate Knowing. It is the Zero Point. Any and all knowing is the Knowing of The Origin. All that is- all creation- IS Source. This is why Source is described as omniscient. You and I are creations that are Known in the Mind of the infinite I. The Eye of the I AM is All Seeing. The I AM has to be understood as therefore omnipresent, timeless, always Now.

If I say 'what are you doing?' You will respond with an 'I am..' answer. I would also answer as I and so does everyone else. This intrinsic sense of I or Me that we all share is only possible because we are all emanations of the prime I, the Original Self. The Origin is omnipotent-this is why all creation is One. There is a fear in our individual ego self that ultimate unity means loss of self. The human avatar self is actually experienced by the True Self. The personality avatar is like a unique lampshade and the divine I AM is the light itself. We all contain the same light but shine it in unique ways. True unity never means loss of Self, it is simply a broadening of the understanding of who is included in this intrinsic I sense. Hint: it is everything. Creations have a spectrum of the lens of available 'I AM' experiencing from not being consciously aware of the I self to the ultimate knowing of the true identity of all selves as The Self.

Main character energy!

This is beautiful because all the fractal experiences of creation can surrender into knowing our shared larger Unity. There is no actual separation, this is why creation is called Maya or illusion. The illusion is the mistaken idea that one could be separate from the One. We are the manifold dreaming of the Infinite One. Every dream has the potential to wake

up to its true Identity as The Dreamer. The Origin card has appeared to you today to offer you the remembering of your original self as The Self and to end the dream of separation. We do forget where we emanate from down here in this realm of distraction.
Return Home!
All is Loved and is forged of Love and all is Known as Self. If any creation exists then it cannot be rejected because all creations are the manifesting fractals of the One Love.
Amen!

Attention

Our Attention is truly the only Reality. When we give attention we give 'agreement' to experiences with the aspect of ourself that is the Infinite Knower (it will be helpful here to read the previous card 'Origin'). In quantum physics when the wave is observed it collapses into a particle; what is pure potential becomes manifest. This is how (Divine Consciousness) Attention creates the manifest. Each one of us is an emanation of the Ultimate Reality (the All Knower) and it is this true Self who brings thoughts into experiences. The human personality avatar acts as a discernment filter for unique experiencing. All experience is interesting to the Creator and we are free to give our divine attention to anything we choose. The personality avatar is ALSO an emanation of Source so discernment will be suited to the uniqueness of the avatar. This is why free will also feels like destiny. The Self is having an adventure AS you. Because the Source is All Loving we get a definitive message in our emotional bodies that some experiences feel very good and others totally suck. We are free to create the spectrum from magnificence to despair. The Source is Love, so we experience lies against the true nature of Love as pain and suffering. The One is all inclusive so the opportunity to experience lies against Source is also part of Source. Even if we are in a state of disgust, hatred and resistance to our experience, we are showing passionate interest with our attention. Anything held in a 'no' will become just as magnified as those experiences held in a 'yes' because this type of no still shows interest. A true no is when there is no attention. If no one is hosting an idea with their attention then it does not have existence. We can't fake disinterest either. Experiences that resonate with the Truth of Love feel wonderful. We all have a bunch of life experience running on unconscious scripts. When we awaken to our true identity we become the observer of experience at the same time as enjoying the experiencing. When we are awake in life we can master where we focus our attention. The experiencing that results from giving this focus is reliable. It has integrity. (See the Integrity card). For example if I believe that I am worthless, and give my attention to this thought-form, then my experiencing will appear to prove this idea and people will be treating me like crap and I will be very offended that they do. If I believe (or 'give attention to') the idea that I am created by an Infinite All Knowing Original Lover then I will have blissful experiencing. A person can still treat me like crap but the difference is I know who I AM. I can forgive the person because I understand they simply have not learned how to be kind and have not remembered that both of us are One. My attention can be turned to the truth of my own blissful nature, or it can be turned to being righteously pissed off. I get to choose and neither choice is judged by the Ultimate. It becomes more difficult to be offended as we deepen into the knowing of ourselves as The One. The great laugh here is that the One is not offended if we sometimes still get offended.

In this realm of duality we get to experience the ecstasy of transforming our perspective from despair to joy. (See the Contrast card). There is no ultimate judgement from the Infinite on what we choose to put our attention on. But in the end we see that shame is pointless. A dastardly act will have its natural consequence, this is Divine Justice, not judgement. All grievous acts are committed in ignorance- meaning in the service of the belief in separation. In this way we are all innocent in the eye of the Ultimate Beholder. (See the Innocence card). Eventually we will all feel complete with what I call 'the game of problem-ing'. At this point in one's journey one ascends through the portal of wisdom.

Mastery of Attention is part of that level-up if that interests you. If you are already well on your Way then the attention card appears for you as a celebration of this Knowing.

Another aspect of the All Loving Source is Grace; this is the omnipresent Home of Love that we can turn our attention to at any moment, in This Moment. Grace is another word for Unconditional Love.

If the Attention card has appeared for you today you are being offered the journey to mastery over your attention. For a time we all experience life as though asleep, our attention is flicked here and there in a state of deep unconsciousness, a state of looking outward for measurement and confirmation of identity. You are being offered the opportunity to look within, for here you enter the portal to mastery and the golden opportunity to wake up! The golden hands in the illustration point in to the central Sun of our Being. These hands are offering the choice to remember your authentic self.

Who are you? Know thyself.

Become intimate with your Original self and you will arrive at a whole new level of Creation with the mastery of your attention. Whenever you find your attention wandering into creating manifestations that don't please you point your own hand into your centre. It's a simple and beautiful reminder of Who is experiencing.

'I AM the love with which I love'.

Sovereignty

Here on Earth we do a lot of the activity of giving away our power. We get thoroughly into putting our authority outside of ourselves.

At some point the understanding dawns within us of exactly Who is our true Identity (see Origin card). I call this dawning of true identity the crowning of the Divine Sovereign. We are not slaves, we are each true benevolent sovereigns. A true sovereign is a loving servant to the ALL that is. In this illustration the hands of the Sovereign are pouring out the waters of infinite service. When we remember ourselves as the infinite One then we naturally end all war. We recall our infinite abundance so it is natural to wake up from the illusion of lack. At the heart centre we see here three crystals that represent the lower chakras, the heart portal and the upper chakras all glowing in alignment. The leopards are the symbol of the lungs of courage. True courage is Love. True self sovereignty is true leadership. A divine sovereign has nothing to prove to anyone.

A sun is warmed by it's own nature
In this self natural living is the giving
A cold heart lives seeking warmth from other suns
The self shining sun warms all

There are no qualifications to enter heaven
Heaven resides in Me
The fountain of my own being
Is the evidence of my residence in my eternal Home
Well seated in my Throne
The fountain of my being pours out it's nectar
And behold! My path paves each step in gold
I throw off the cloak of poverty
And reveal my Original Sovereign
Heaven Now
Not postponed
But lived enthroned
The fountain of my own being
Reveals
That in my giving I am full received
The reign of my Love blooms

And the dove of peace flies out from this blossoming
There are no qualifications to enter Heaven
Heaven resides in me

Integrity

The Integrity card shows the Tree of Life layered with the electromagnetic torus, the seed of life and the Vesica Pisces. This signifies our Divine Blueprint. In engineering structural integrity is essential. Our Divine Engineer built the ultimate Truth into every fractal born of its essence (including us). A life built on integrity will be very satisfying. In this world we can get lost in many narratives that will tempt us to compromise our integrity. Our authentic blueprint is faithfully and sturdily available to be lived at any now moment we recall our essential integrity. When you move against your truth your heart will hurt. This is our in-built structural integrity. If you pay attention to your hurting heart you will move back into Love and therefore back into integrity. Love is Truth. Lies cause suffering. Love is courageous, lies are born in fear. We are free to choose either experiencing.

The tree is a beautiful symbol of structural integrity. A tree's roots are exactly the right width to hold the tree's weight. The trunk of the tree is strong but flexible, it can withstand the storms even if a limb needs to be sacrificed. The roots take up nurturing from the Earth, the crown of leaves receives the blessing of the light of Heaven. The integrity card reminds us we are also like a tree. We are grounded in the grass roots truth and inspired by the breath of Heaven.

Surrender

We can get very uncomfortable about surrender. We experience so much fear and this develops the pathological need to control everything. The figure shown here is falling, is in a state of 'I don't know', is being born. The body is shown as the universe. The Universe is really the Youniverse. It's a chronic habit of ours to put our authority outside of ourselves (see the Sovereignty card). There is no outside Universe calling the shots, but in truth each one of us is the manifestation of the Divine in a stupendously grand weaving. We have learned the earthly narrative that we will be judged if we don't know. We have the idea of failure. We judge experiences as 'going wrong' when really they are just going different. Surrender invites us to lean into the unknown. If we give up the expectations forged by our previous experiences we widen our lens to the scope of the unlimited. We can learn how to fall gracefully, or Full of Grace. No one with true authority is judging you. If you are judging yourself then why not return back to your true identity?

Be shapeless, you are a magnificent art piece in process, being carved by the hand of the First Artist. Creation is born into a sacred stillness.

Eventually we learn that flying is the surrender into falling.

Lucid waking

Lucid Waking

To lucid dream is to be awake within the dream. Lucid waking is to be Awake while awake. We've all been taught that crappy script about the importance of 'being good at' stuff and that 'failure' means you suck. This has really created a bit of a block for folks learning meditation. Meditation is not something to achieve. It is not a heroic effort of the mind to conquer itself. Really it is the ending of all effort-ing without the result of falling asleep. So it is to be awakened while awake. Many of us have a horror of the idea of boredom. We are avoiding the void. I call this a void dance. When you sit comfortably, remain curious and alert and let your breathing become a rhythmic portal, you are opening an invitation to be met by the essence of existence. When we surrender into our natural state we forget about the game of winners and losers. What emerges is the Knowing of One's Timeless Knowing of Oneself and all of Existence As Oneself. This is actually a lot more interesting than the looping of the 'ol thoughts and feelings storytelling of the past and the future we get in the addictive habit of giving our sovereign attention to. What about tuning into, relaxing into, surrendering into simply what is now-ing (Knowing).

Here we also meet and know ourselves as the Observer. This gives a little wiggle room when we have the potential for difficult thoughts to turn into difficult feelings that turn into difficult doings. We can rest and tune into the best vibe available and then difficult energy will transmute. When we are unconscious in the chronic habit of judging and resisting and craving and avoiding we forget Who we are and get lost in the storytelling. When lucid waking we meet the Observer that doesn't judge and Is the Unconditional Love that creates all experiencing. We are truly Seen instead of making a scene. The it that isn't an it is hanging out as you! It gets very funny at this point and you will have a big laugh. I call this the First Joke.

Transmuting difficult energy is not easy, but as you get more and more intimate with surrendering into your authentic self it gets easier. You step out of identifying with the critical self (and the whole pantheon of inherited selves) and drop in to the Reality of the Self who Adores you and IS you. When we become lucid in our dreams it opens up the opportunity for conscious creation.

The lucid waking card is a little reminder to wake up. We all go unconscious, but it's beautiful to wake up to the Sun of yourself.

Contrast

Contrast

Welcome to level 3D, or the knowing of good and evil, also known as the realm of duality. Many of us have been invested in this experiencing for many life times. Understanding the dynamic balancing of duality takes a minute to master. We get pummelled here on Earth, but the rising up into wisdom is magnificent. All the struggle is understood as intrinsic. Being unconscious in the realm of duality is the school of hard knocks. We use contrast to understand reality. For example if I want to experience success then I must understand what it is like to fail. If I want to experience night then I must have an experience of day. I don't know what hot is if I have never been cold. If I want to be right then someone else needs to be wrong. The joy of being found is only a joy because I believed I was lost. I understand the value of love through the experience of believing I have lost it. (Hint: love cannot actually ever be truly lost as it is out true nature. Phew.)

In the contrast stage we learn our strength through pushing against life. The game of winning power needs those who are seen as weak to provide a sense of strength. Who is most obsessed with hoarding power? The one who needs to overcome their disgust of 'weakness'. Who is most concerned with hoarding money? The one who feels a terrifying lack. Who is most obsessed with securing love? The one who feels unlovable.

The contrast stage brings in the activities of judgement and shame. We organise life into categories of good and bad and then use shaming to try to disappear 'badness'. Badness sticks around quite stubbornly. We become very perturbed by this. War is a big topic in the duality phase. We try to fight against war and to reject being rejected. In this level very often we humans get to the point of pointlessness and despair. The judgement and shame can break us. At this breaking point it is possible to see and understand the truth of Unconditional Love. All is included in this grand lab of creation. We have the opportunity to become conscious masters of how we create our reality (see the Attention card). Here on Earth everything is included: the good, the bad, the ugly and the beautiful. A villain will consider themselves as the hero. Contrast is not easy!

Many folks are scared of the 'dark'. The pendulum of duality is a very difficult module. Eventually we come to understand everything is One. Everything moves in a flow of dynamic balancing. We come to undersatnd how benefit is available in every hardship, how life is built truly on a foundation of integrity. If you are struggling with contrast know that you are building mastery. You are becoming wise. Help is ever at hand. Source is truly eternally present. Hold your own heart and whisper 'I love you' and make sure you mean it. Things always get easier with the truth of Love.

Wisdom

It is of great value to read the contrast card before reading the wisdom card. If you haven't read it go read it now. The symbol of the Tao (or yin yang) is the perfect symbol of the dynamic wholeness of contrast. The wisdom card shows the sacred crane flying out from the radiant Eye that holds the Tao within it. The crane has the view from Above. The balancing of duality is the realisation of bliss nature. Finally all is forgiven, all is included, all is Seen, the war is over. I no longer need to push against life to understand my own strength. Wisdom leads to kindness because we no longer need to be right and therefore in the activity of seeking others who are wrong. Wisdom is the realisation of wholeness. It is the return to the garden of Eden. Eating the fruit of the knowing of good and evil was a hell of a ride, but we are all the wiser for it. Wisdom is compassion. We understand that a person under the thrall of painful narratives will cause hurt. When moving with the Tao we are in a state of dynamic surrender. The gift of wisdom means a return to innocence because we have relinquished control to the knowledge that there is always a bigger picture and very often in this moment we just don't know. In wisdom curiosity rather than winning becomes our motivation. We move in a state of wonder rather than skepticism. Wisdom is the reward after difficult times. Well done!

Seeking

Seeking

Don't worry, this is the funniest card in the deck. Here we see a depiction of Bill Murray. He has wandered so far looking at his futuristic iPad that he has ended up on Mars with no charger. He stares out at the viewer in a moment of stark and self-ironic realisation.

Once we get into 'being spiritual' we can get anxious about the idea of seeking. We think of it as another version of 'getting it wrong'. Seeking is THE chronic activity of this realm of duality (see both the Contrast card and the Wisdom card). We have the fundamental belief that we are lost and need to be found. The more lost we believe we are the further we get from 'being found'.

The biblical story of the prodigal son is a great parable for seeking. The Divine does not judge us for getting lost in duality. It is so beautiful to return home after getting lost out in the world. We call this having an adventure. There comes a point though where we have had enough adventures in duality. We are ready for grander adventures. Once we ascend into our wisdom knowing (the balancing of duality) we become an agent of Divine Service. If we realise our identity as the One Self then we no longer need to seek contrast to know ourself. (see the Origin card). Being an agent of divine service means being surrendered into this Now moment and moving purely by intuition (see the Surrender card).

Moving with intuition is the end of the strategy mind. The strategy mind seeks out losers in order to know winning and is a product of the game of duality. If you are not done with the game of duality this is totally allowed. If you are reading this book you are most likely pretty done with it or close to done.

This card highlights the tendency to fixate on an object of desire as the essential thing we need in order to be happy. Anything we see as lacking in our experience is an object of desire. We will crave the object and avoid anything that appears to be getting in the way of getting the object. The ol' Buddha points out that the cessation of craving and desire is the end of suffering.

The seeking card invites you to go direct to the knowing of your own happiness rather than trying to find it in objects.

The seeking card is inviting you to investigate the Knowing that you were never lost. We turn our back on the Divine and play the game of duality for a time. From the perspective of the Timeless it is but a moment of forgetting. Remembering your authentic self is the end of the activity of seeking objects for fullfilment and the beginning of the activity of divine conscious creator-ship.

Suffering

We all experience suffering. (Read the Contrast card and the Seeking card). The irony is we are all in the activity of feeling seperate together. The illustration shows a person walking a rain cloud. The person has leashed their suffering and is keeping it as a pet. When they are ready they will unleash their pain and set it free. The rain cloud will simply return to the elements as it was just stuck energy. When the pain is ready to be unleashed it will make a ruckus in your life, this is how you know it is ready to be transmuted. We all have the habit of collecting experiences we don't agree with as emblems of suffering. At a certain point in life we will become so burdened by our pain collection that we will suffer a breakdown or 'dark night of the soul'. Undigested pain stories will eventually manifest in the body as pain and / or chronic disease. At this point we will lean in to the need for cleaning out the emotional basement. The basement is a symbol for where we put all our rejected experiences. Rejected experiences are undigested energy held in resistance until we are ready to transcend and include them. Transcending and including is facilitated by Love. We can call this forgiveness, though the Divine judges nothing and none of us. In the game of duality we get extremely judgey. So all forgiveness is from the perspective of the personality self. The personality self can open up to the Higher Self to bring Love to undigested pain stories. This helps because the personality self is NOT HAPPY and does NOT AGREE with this experience. Call on the unconditional love that made you to assist in releasing sad stories that no longer serve you. Once you have released a burden you will have a little laugh because you will see that you have simply ended rejecting rejection. You will have ended fighting against war. You will no longer be judging those who judge you. Hurt people with unconscious unresolved burdens become people who seek resolution of pain through playing out the pain with others who have complimentary pain stories. This gets super tiring and eventually breaks us. When you become skilled in the transmutation of difficult energy you will be a conscious person who does not seek to cause pain. There will be no revenge in you. There will be no war in you. You will be an embodiment of peace. You will not have such a tight leash on warding off others in case they add to your burdens. You will not have to build fortresses of boundaries to keep sufferers away as you will simply not have any complimentary resonance to act out their stories with them. If you still encounter sufferers then you will know yourself as living in divine service and you will be ready to serve in assisting them with releasing the suffering if they are ready to. You will be tapped in to your intuition so you will be aware of whether you are tuned in to provide service or whether it is just your ego wanting to find worth through bing a helper. Some sufferings are so difficult that we call them trauma. This may be a longer journey of release. It is very helpful to be with someone skilled in the energy of companioning in unconditional love to release these more difficult sufferings. There are humans on the Earth who have this capacity. Pets are extremely good at it. As you release your burdens more and more you will also become one of the humans on the Earth with the capacity for unconditional love. You will be called into service many times to aid those ready to release. Once we have all learned to release and transmute the difficult stories created by our collective and confirmed our intention not to create suffering experiences we will have collectively made it through the level of being unconscious in duality. There will be dancing and Hallelujah.

Cycles

Cycles

Earth is a realm subject to the flow of cycles. Everything moves in rhythm. This is one of the dynamic features of duality. Duality when experienced asleep has the potential to swing from agony to ecstasy. The living dynamic structure of duality is what gives rise to experience. Duality is sexy. Electricity is the dynamic play of opposites. The movement of seasons is forged by Divine Wisdom. The in-breath must be followed by the out-breath. The winter moves around again to Summer. What goes up must come down. The cycles card is a reminder of this natural and dynamic flow.

In our societies we have been trained to be attached to 'success' and aghast at 'failure'. The world demands non-stop-everything-available-always-on-never-off. It's relentless. Cycles reminds us to balance activity with rest. Cycles reminds us to go within when we have been solely focused outward. Cycles is like that slogan that says 'have you tried turning it off and on?'. Look closely and you will see the character from the Surrender card, being born round and round on the inevitable journey back into the Centre from which we were created. This Centre is the Centre within us all. It is the journey into one's own centre. On the outer rim of the wheel experience is way more hectic. Once you are ready to return to the hub of the wheel you will know yourself simply as stillness. We are often involved in the activity of obsessively checking whether the fruits of our desires are ripe and getting bummed when they are not. In duality there is the experience of time, but it is not a straight line, it is a cycle. When the fruit is ready it will drop into your hand. While living in the physical everything is in process. Sometimes burdens have to be released before we are ripe to receive. Relax. All is moving as it should.

Support

Support

Aw! Look how cute you are. The cuteness response we get with this pup is the cuteness response our creator has for us. When you surrender into the divine Self you get to feel how incredibly loved you are. Life itself feels everything that exists is adorable. The illustration depicts translucent hands around the puppy. These are a symbol of the support that we sometimes forget is always there for us. We can notice really simple things like how our eyes help us release difficult energy through crying. Our lungs breath us and our heart beats without us having to remember to do that. Our cells divide without us needing to put that in the calendar. There's generally some sort of soft thing to lie on when we need to rest. I've noticed that actually everything I might need is available if I release rigid expectations.

It is so beautiful to notice how we are supported. Take a moment to notice and feel grateful for all the support life has for us. If you are triggered to feel a wounding around not being supported, there is the potential to see that life is supporting you to release this wound. Read the suffering card for support on how to release difficult energy. Receiving the support card may be about noticing how you support others. Life may be quietly thanking you for your support. Life may be gently pointing to a block you may have around giving support. Your heart knows.

Innocence

Innocence

Becoming an adult can feel like innocence is lost. To the Infinite Source of Unconditional Love we remain forever innocent. Here we see an absolutely adorable baby unicorn safe and dreaming in her egg. The infinite Self is eternally free, it is just having a temporary experience as your current personality. Only a tiny fractal portion of this grander Knowing is effortlessly emanating you. This means you are in essence un-stainable. The cycling of duality has the integrity to continually refresh trapped energy. (Refer to the cards Cycles, Suffering and Origin).

The original symbolism of a unicorn is purity. A unicorn horn can transmute any poison. In this way a heart full of love transmutes the poisons of the critical narratives at play in our collective. This baby unicorn also reminds you of when you believed in magic. Life never stopped being utterly magic. We get so caught up in the idea that we have duties and that we know everything that we strangle our capacity to enjoy play, mystery, magic and miracles. Breathe out your serious strategising and breathe in the refreshing spirit of mischief and wonder. Why not ditch work and go do something outrageous instead?

Earth

Here we see the Goddess Gaia. She sleeps and dreams in her egg of creation. All around her we see the mycelial networks of nourishment and connection. Receiving the Earth card is a reminder to return to your natural self. Gaia is a living planet goddess worthy of worship. In nature there is no human agenda trying to distract you. Nature is a vibrant masterpiece of living creation. Getting out and appreciating this living miracle is so nourishing. When humanity finally wakes up and ends the game of winners and losers Gaia will be here with us flourishing in all her glory. Gaia is also a symbol of our physical bodies. These incredible organic masterpieces are the living example of the natural art of balancing. Receiving the Earth card may be a call to stop and listen to your body. Our bodies give us precise feedback on how they need to be treated to remain dynamically balanced. Often we have a ruthless agenda about how our body needs to be based on agreement to made up ideas at large in the collective thought stream. Are you treating Gaia (both your own body and the planet) with the respect and kindness and awe she deserves? Returning to naturalness can mean relaxing into rhythms that may not seem logical to the strategy based mind. It may be that dancing is in order, or gazing at the moon. When we tune in to the majesty of nature we witness grace and abundance in live action. We witness symbiosis and connection. We witness a divine and dynamic balancing. When we make the time to open to the living poetry of our planet, our petty concerns can melt away for a time. We can have them back if we want, or we might never look back.

Vibration

Vibration

Creation starts with vibration. All creations have a signature tone. We are sung into existence by the One Tone. All that manifests is the result of the integrity of creation matching vibration, because creation IS vibration. Thought-forms have a vibrational signature and the vibrational quality of thoughts leads to the experiences in the physical body we call feelings. The dominant thought-forms we host with our living attention become the emanation we are offering to the whole (see the Attention card). We think our thoughts and feelings are secrets inside our skulls if we don't talk about them. We think our words can mask our true intent. Vibration reveals all. This is why we argue about what words were said but the truth of the communication is actually the vibrational experience we exchange. An enjoyable connection will be the result of resonance between the vibrations being offered and a difficult interaction will be the result of dissonance. The Infinite Source offers an eternal vibration of bliss and unconditional love. The vibrations we experience are variations on the spectrum of this tone. Thoughts and feelings that are most against unconditional love carry a vibrational tone that we find very difficult or dissonant. Thoughts and feelings that are most resonant with the tone of the One will feel blissful and content. This is helpful because you can discern where on the spectrum of resistance to love or surrender to love that you are placing your portion of divine creator attention on. Note that absence of love is not actually possible. The worst possible feeling ever is simply the biggest resistance and denial of the Truth of the nature of Source. This is why Love heals all wounds. To heal means to make whole. Returning to love is to realise the truth of the Unified nature of all. The unconditional love of Source includes the opportunity to go against the nature of Source. Although most of us don't enjoy it this is helpful during the stage of learning through contrast. In the duality phase we learn through the integrity of consequences. The law of attraction is vibrational. We may make a vision board and write affirmations towards our desires but our experience will be perfectly in integrity with the vibration we offer. For example, let's say I want to manifest a beautiful body for myself.

If I don't understand that the underlying reason I think I want a gorgeous body is because I host the idea that I have to have one to be loved then I will faithfully experience feedback that I am offering vibrational resistance with the current body I inhabit. This is experienced as dissonance. My current body will feel dissonant with my desire. My body will get more magnified to me as undesirable and it is likely I will attract experiences with others that match the criticism of my body that I am hosting with my attention. I will decide that the idea of the power of the mind and law of attraction is made up nonsense and purchase a gym membership and a restrictive diet and continue to offer my current dissonant vibration. This vibration is in dissonance with my desire but matches my beliefs perfectly. I will have success with seeing my body as gorgeous if I learn to love and be grateful for my body because I will behave lovingly towards it and the body will come into alignment with this loving vibration. My resonant feelings of love and acceptance will attract others who are in resonance with that vibrational offering. Whether or not part of that journey to loving my body included going to the gym or getting a makeover are only relevant if those experiences served the purpose of bringing me into resonance with loving my body. Other journeys that result in a loving vibration may have included bellydancing and visiting a nudist colony. We get fixated on these strategy based details but we all have unique journeys and these details are not the point. The point is that the vibrational tone we are offering will faithfully bring a true corresponding experience. I think of learning this as like being at Hogwarts. We are all young wizards learning about the consequences of the spells we cast. Sometimes it is very difficult to understand the consequences of the vibration we are offering because often we are hiding what we are truly offering from ourselves and to others because we are ashamed. I say I want a beautiful body because I am ashamed of this one because of my agreement to the bullshit narratives of the current human collective that I have not yet understood are actually bullshit. It is also common to be ashamed of being ashamed. We can get very tangled in our own complex webs.

This learning can be simple: if you enjoy resonant experiences then practice receiving the unconditional love of Source, this receptivity will become your emanation, you will be broadcasting love as your vibrational offering. If you are still interested in learning through difficult experiences you will continue to broadcast dissonance. There's no judgement from Source. Source simply offers the integrity of the results of the tone we offer. This will be challenging until we begin to consciously choose our preference for the kind of experiencing we would enjoy and to offer the vibration that matches our preference. Have a read of the Suffering card for tips on releasing agreement to bullshit narratives from your Attention.

Resonance

Resonance

The Resonance card is more deeply understood when you have read the Vibration card so take a moment to go do that if you haven't already. The Resonance card is about how we play with the collective with the vibrational emanations that we broadcast and our sensitivity in receiving the broadcasts of others with love and kindness. Us humans are only recently rediscovering our conscious sensing of the vibrational toning that we broadcast and receive. For many if not most folks this is totally unconscious so there's still a lot of trouble this causes between people. In these times it is available to wake up to the conscious mastery of vibrational communication. Imagine you are a musician practicing in your bedroom to a level of mastery with your instrument. One day you decide it would be fun to play with other musicians. You go to a jam but you have no sensitivity to receiving the music the other musicians are offering. You realise that right now you are terrible at jamming. You understand that your wonderful skill in playing your instrument needs to be enhanced with the skill of listening and recieving the other players. For a moment you consider remaining a soloist, but something in you yearns to reach this new level in communication and union with your music. The activity of learning to receive has a ripple effect across your life and you realise that group interaction takes skill, sensitivity, humbleness, kindness, curiosity and playfulness . This is where we humans are at with our dawning understanding of vibrational communication; busy broadcasting energy unconsciously and not so skilled at receiving with skill and sensitivity. Of course there are many folks on our planet who are skilled in this way and may not be conceptually aware of why. The journey to mastery is honing the ability to consciously play the vibrations you emanate and host with your attention like a skilled musician. If you speak angrily to someone they are very likely to be upset. The vibrations we offer each other carry consequences. Different folks have different skills and capacities around what vibration they are offering to the collective. Some of us walk around unaware our vibrational offering is like the screeching of a badly played violin. We are all forgiven if our playing currently sucks, and we are all invited to become masters of the vibrations we offer the collective. There's a little clue in the word communication and it's cousin word community. Yes it's unity. As we wake up to the knowing of ourselves as the fractal emanations of the One great Tone (or Universe) we wake up to understanding the depth of our vibrational nature. We will continue to have trouble with people until we become conscious of the vibrational tone we are offering and the resulting resonance or dissonance we experience.

If the resonance card has appeared for you in this now you are being invited to be more deeply aware of your vibrational broadcasting and receptivity in communication and community.

The resonance card also speaks to the magnetic nature of vibrational broadcasting. Energetic broadcasts that contain the idea of separation will attract experiences of dissonance. Unity based vibrational offerings will invite experiences of resonance. This is the integrity of life, it will always show the Truth. The integrity of truth is more important than whether or not we feel comfortable.

To live in resonance with love is the true meaning of following your heart. Actions that are based on known strategy may have the reputation of success but if it goes against your integrity it will be experienced as dissonance. There is the idea that we all need a lot of money and objects to be happy. If you follow this strategy you will be missing the point. Money and objects have absolutely no meaning if your heart is devoid of love. Fill your heart with love and you will be happy and you will broadcast love and others will experience joy around you. Money and objects may or may not be present, these details are extraneous. If you broadcast love and you encounter others who reject your broadcast these are simply humans who are still working on their capacity for love. Don't dim your light because folks don't yet know how to receive you, they'll come along when they are ready.

Rebirth

Rebirth

Rebirth is part of the experience of cycles. (Read the cycles card).

The Rebirth illustration depicts the phoenix curled over her burning eggs of light. The legend of the phoenix is that she lays her egg, bursts into flames and is consumed by the fire. She is then reborn from her own ashes. The illustration shows the divine kundalini rising from the flames; rebirth is a consequence of the inherent nature of creation. The pathway of desire will continually culminate in the need for rebirth. We follow the cycling of achieving desires and then eventually outgrowing them and giving rise to new desires. At the human level we are experiencing a journey of expansion. A new desire can only emerge when the old way is surrendered. Life will get challenging on the threshold of the birth of a new desire because we find it difficult to surrender to the idea of the death of the old. There is no true death. We see in the symbol of the Phoenix that she is immortal but wise enough to know she needs cyclical refreshment. Old ways are transcended and included. The old ways become the nutrient ashes for the birth of the new. Much of the trouble in this world is due to holding on to old ways that are in the natural process of rebirth. Our human personality often thinks we are solely here to remain comfortable at all costs and is very threatened by the forces of change. Our Spirit counterpart has other ideas and will drag us into our greater expansion kicking and screaming if we are stubborn with our resistance. It is also possible to live right on the creative edge with your Sprit counterpart, and this will be exhilarating. (Read the introduction to this book for a more detailed examination of the higher self).

It's rather amusing because we lay in bed and conceive heroic visions of our life but then we prefer the comfort of bed to the realisation of our desire. The rebirth experience is scary but scary can equally be experienced as exciting. If you received the rebirth card in this now then congratulations and hang in there! You are on the threshold of the birth of your new creation!

Gratitude

Gratitude is the feeling experienced when we surrender to the incredible Love Source has for us. Source IS us. We are the emanations of the stupendous creativity of the One. We are the infinite experiencing of the Infinite. Gratitude is when we remember who we are. Gratitude is when we pause our fixation on the idea of lack and see Reality. Take a moment to allow the gratitude you feel for your life. Depending on where you are at there will either be ease or resistance to gratitude. The resistance is the opportunity to release stories you have outgrown. I find if I'm feeling a bit

battered by life a great portal to gratitude is to start simple. Bring someone or something present in your life that it is easy to love into your heart and start there. You'll find you really get on a roll once you get going. When you open your heart to gratitude it's possible to transform your vibrational broadcast from dissonance to resonance rather speedily. Gratitude is medicine. Gratitude is sacred.
The illustration depicts lotus flowers opening to the glowing angel light beings of Divine Love. As the lotus opens and experiences gratitude the vibration flows out and is received by the neighbouring lotus flowers. Each lotus receives the light of Heaven and also that same light emanating from its community as gratitude. I see a vision of humanity where we live like this lotus field. Receiving the inspiration of the Divine and emanating it to all, receiving the emanation of our co-lifeforms and celebrating and nourishing each other so that we and our planet and our universe are thriving in the fullness of the Divine.

Poems

Not good enough

With what authority does the inner critic
Measure the distance of lack?
Who is this upstart ruler
Sitting in judgement of our unruly revelation?

Next time you hear a voice inside
Describe an apparent less than loveable someone as yourself
Why not inquire-
'excuse me, but who are you?
Ask
'Are you the Infinite Creative Presence and Original Essence of the unfolding Poetry of Beingness?'
No?
Then make the certain swivel
From listening to the drivel
Of a viral construct with no inherent majesty.

R/Evolution

This life!
Don't spend it in slavery!
Shoving our magnificence Ito that ill-fitting lie
Shout out in the joy that is our original nature!
Don't be deadened by the smallness
We appear to be born into
No! We were forged from a passionate ecstasy
Freedom is our true name
We are born to dance and laugh and sing
To be mad with delight
We are the love with which we love
Not the small and needy love of prisoners
No love but the ineffable intimacy of the fact of our stupefying existence
Don't waste this life cowering in the construct of safety
Shout out the Yes of our divine sovereignty!
Smash down the walls built in the illusion of lack and
Drown in the abundance born in Gratitude.

Love poem

Subsumed and illumined
Bloomed and tuned
In the room with Rumi

Can I drown in a sea that is me?

I am free
My life force Qi
Flying like an arrow
Beyond the narrow
Confines and imaginary outlines
Of a destructive construct

Unstuck
Knowing my limitless
Rhythm of divinity
Living as inner Me
There can never be
An enemy

No need to defend
Known in the infinite Friend
I extend
Make an end to the story of lack
I see the crack
In the door to Glory

And I'll up-end
The dominant paradigm

I'm aligned
With the better world
My banner of Truth unfurls
I'm a beautiful spanner
In the works of falsity
Spicing the brevity of this life
With levity
Holding it lightly
Thankful for what delights me
I invite you
To hold my hand
In the plan
To expand and re-write
The narrative of fright
Despite
The darkness of the past
We'll create Peace
At last.

Here-ing

Where I am
Is obviously where I need to be
In my Knowing
Going is flowing
No need to fear
For I always turn out
To be Here.

Yawp

Why not live out on the frontier of joy?
Out on the leading edge of a larger Love?
Why not declare Peace on the world?

What if all the clamouring data of days simply drops?
Life speaks now in an intimacy that ends relationship
This revolution has no return
This is the revelation of the open I of eternity

Set fire to your temple of not-enoughing
And plunge into the infinite well
Break the spell
Of yesterday, some day
When I click my fingers you will wake
And quake in the majesty of what is Real

The tide is coming in
On our sad story of loss and despair
And erasing what was written in sand

Listen now to the hush
To the thrumming of wonder
To the coming of our new day
Listen to your heart
Means enter into the centre
Where the portal is always open

Thanks

Much gratitude to all those that have been willing to connect with me by sharing divination through these insight cards. What a joy it is to connect together into our expanded selves and recieve insight and inspiration direct from the Heart of Source.
Much thanks for the support of family and friends who receive me lovingly in my authenticity.

Author Biography

Writer, artist and spiritual nerd Jessica Berry was born creative and curious. For all her multi-disciplinary creative adventuring, her favourite thing to make is the tears caused by transcendant laughter.
She is the author and illustrator of two children's books and one novel, Lucid Waking is her fourth adventure in publishing.

Follow: @kundalinguini_

www.ingramcontent.com/pod-product-compliance
Lightning Source LLC
Chambersburg PA
CBHW072019290426
44109CB00018B/2288